Always Kiss with your Whiskers

Love Advice from my Cat

Liz Nickles and Tamara Asseyer

Illustrated by Bonnie Timmons

POCKET BOOKS

New York   London   Toronto   Sydney   Tokyo   Singapore

An *Original* Publication of Pocket Books

POCKET BOOKS, a division of Simon & Schuster Inc.
1230 Avenue of the Americas, New York, NY 10020

ISBN: 0-671-74983-8

First Pocket Books trade paperback printing November 1991

10 9 8 7 6 5 4 3 2

POCKET and colophon are registered trademarks of
Simon & Schuster Inc.

Cover art by Bonnie Timmons

Printed in the U.S.A.

Are you loved? Unloved? In love? Out of love? Looking for love? ALWAYS KISS WITH YOUR WHISKERS gives the cat's meow in love advice. Who could be luckier in love than someone who lives for petting, purrs louder than a dishwasher, and is professionally lovable? Without saying a word, cats tell us what they think. Now it's up to us to follow their lead.

Bumper

Table of Contents

CHAPTER 1

Meeting

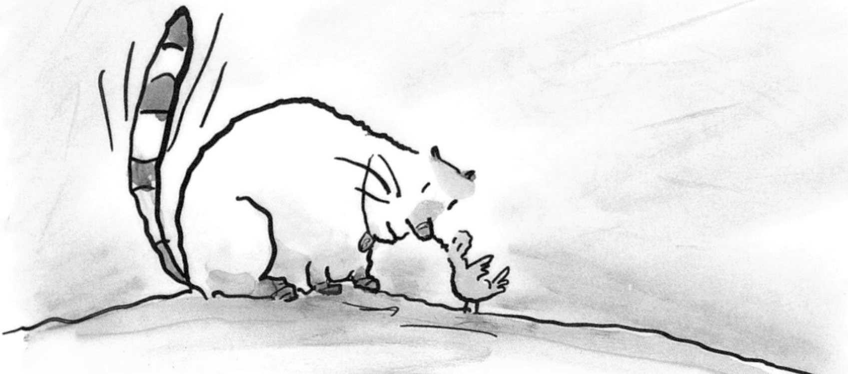

Put your best foot forward

← Bumper

← Button

Look as cute as a button

Use Mouthwash

Practice what you would say to him

Practice how you would really, actually KISS him

CHAPTER 2

Courting

Send love notes

Maintain your mystique

Develop a sensuous stretch

Know your erogenous zones

Romantic dinners should be
tasted in advance

Know when
to be
unavailable

Feign
indifference

Play hard
to get

Wish he would
JUST CALL

How to handle the competition...
1. Ignore

How to handle the competition...
2. Outwit

How to handle the competition...
3. Intimidate

Dream exclusively of him

Be discreet

Exult in emotion

Don't fall too hard

Always kiss with your whiskers...

or your tongue

CHAPTER 3

Commitment

Drop everything for him

When he's playful, play along

Share your snacks

Don't take over his whole
apartment

Don't go unnoticed

CHAPTER 4

Fighting

Twenty-four hours after he said
he'd call
and didn't

sleep

Eat

sleep

Make sure
the phone's
really working

One week later

Eat

Imagine life in a far distant land

Learn a foreign language

Phone missing persons because you think he might be dead

A LOT later

Catch up
on sleep

Call and hang
up when you
hear his voice

Think
existential
thoughts

Think about
ANYTHING
besides him

Don't get your back up

claws <u>IN</u> paw:

keep your claws in

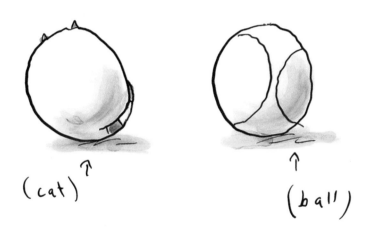

(cat) ↑

(ball) ↑

Curl into a ball

Hold your tongue

Be too cute to be mad at

Never go to bed mad

C H A P T E R 5

Reconciling

Forgive and Forget

Let nothing come between you

Ignore his indiscretions

Risk everything

Regret nothing

CHAPTER 6

Reality

Spend holidays with his family

If he brings home work,
distract him

When wearing black,
accessorize with fur

Have separate bathrooms

When his mother serves pot roast,
ask for seconds

Maintain your independence

Accept his friends

CHAPTER 7
Uh Oh, It's ALL OVER

Become an emotional cripple

Binge

When all else fails,
go shopping

CHAPTER 8

After it's ALL OVER

Remember: He's not the
last man on earth.